Being Patient
with Tapi

by MommyHooray

Your heart can stay steady.
Your breath can soften the moment.
Trust yourself to wait.

This book is loved by

____

BEING PATIENT WITH TAPI
by MommyHooray

Written and published under the pen name MommyHooray.
Illustrations created using digital illustration tools.

Printed in the United States of America.

ISBN: 978-1-972071-62-5

For more stories and updates, visit:
https://sites.google.com/view/mommyhooray/

To the little ones who are learning to wait,
even when it feels hard.

To the deep breaths you take,
the moments you pause,
and the gentle strength growing inside you.

You are doing more than you know.

With Googolplex Love,

You move through moments soft and slow,
Where quiet little wonders grow.
Each pause becomes a gentle space,
A breath, a calm, a steady place.

Are you ready to take your time?

You stand in line and softly sway,
The world keeps moving anyway.
Your moment waits, it will arrive,
No need to rush to feel alive.

Can you enjoy the waiting too?

Waiting
is part
of the
journey.

You breathe in slow, the world feels wide,
A quiet ocean lives inside.
The air moves gently, in and through,
A calm that softly carries you.

Can you feel your breath like a wave?

Your breath is
your anchor.

You take small steps, no need to race,
Each tiny move has gentle grace.
The path unfolds beneath your feet,
Slow journeys feel especially sweet.

What happens when you slow down?

Slow steps
still move you
forward.

You sit in stillness, soft and light,
The hush around you feels just right.
No noise, no rush, just gentle air,
A peaceful pause is waiting there.

What does the quiet sound like to you?

Quiet
holds
hidden
treasures.

A feeling rises, strong and tall,
It moves within, then softens all.
You watch it come, then drift away,
Like waves that roll, then fade to gray.

What helps your feelings feel calmer?

Feelings move like water.

A seed of calm is planted deep,
It grows each time you pause and breathe.
With care and time it starts to rise,
A quiet strength before your eyes.

What is growing inside you?

Patience grows
little by little.

You hold a thought, then let it go,
It floats away, soft and slow.
No need to keep what drifts apart,
Light clouds can lift a heavy heart.

Can you let go of what you don't need?

Letting go
makes space
for calm.

It didn’t work the way you planned,
You pause, then gently try again.
Each little try helps you grow strong,
You’re learning all the way along.

What can you learn from trying again?

Trying again
is courage.

Some things need time to fully bloom,
They won't rush in or fill the room.
You wait, you trust, you let them be,
Time works its quiet mystery.

What can you do while you're waiting?

Good things
take time.

When things feel loud or out of place,
You find your calm, your gentle space.
A steady heart, a softened mind,
A quiet strength you always find.

Where is your calm place?

Calm lives
inside you.

You choose your actions, soft and kind,
With thoughtful care inside your mind.
No need to rush or push ahead,
You follow where your calm has led.

How do you know
when a choice is gentle?

Gentle choices feel right.

A tiny step, a moment bright,
You did your best, and that's just right.
Each little win begins to grow,
More than you may even know.

How did you show patience today?

Small steps
shine big.

You pause your hands, you rest your feet,
The stillness feels so calm and sweet.
No need to move or do or go,
Just being here is all you know.

What do you feel
when you are calm and still?

Stillness is powerful.

You speak with care inside your mind,
Your thoughts are gentle, soft, and kind.
No harsh or hurried words today,
Just quiet warmth along the way.

Can you be kind to yourself?

Kindness starts within.

In every pause, a light appears,
A quiet strength that grows each year.
You hold it softly, calm and bright,
A gentle glow, your inner light.

What helps your patience grow?

Patience is your
quiet superpower.

You took your time, you moved with care,
Found gentle moments everywhere.
Each breath, each pause, each step you take,
Builds peaceful paths for you to make.

How can you keep your calm with you?

A Message From Tapi

Dear Friend,

Sometimes waiting can feel really hard.

But you paused for a moment,
you took a slow, gentle breath,
and you stayed right where you were.

That's how patience begins to grow—
in quiet, everyday moments like these.

You can take your time.
I'm right here with you.

High-fives and Happy Hugs,

Grow with Tapi Series

Small steps. Big growth.

These titles guide children through feelings, challenges, and growth with care, encouragement, and understanding.

Grow together with the Grow with Tapi series, one small moment at a time.

Discover More with Tapi

Learn with Tapi Series

PLANETS with Tapi

COLORS with Tapi

SEASONS and WEATHER with Tapi

JOBS with Tapi

SENSES with Tapi

SHAPES with Tapi
by MommyHooray

LETTERS with Tapi
by MommyHooray

NUMBERS with Tapi
by MommyHooray

KIND WORDS with Tapi
by MommyHooray

FEELINGS with Tapi
by MommyHooray

... and more!

From My Heart to Yours

Write a note, memory, or wish for the child who will treasure this book.

Today's Date: ________________

May this page find you again, years from now.

www.ingramcontent.com/pod-product-compliance
Lightning Source LLC
LaVergne TN
LVHW070156110826
845147LV00002B/415

* 9 7 8 1 9 7 2 0 7 1 6 2 5 *